# Cocktails and Prayers

## A Memoir by
## Dr. Phil Jones

*Bess,*

*You are a great friend.*
*Best wishes to the Richardsons.*

*Phil Jones*

Library of Congress Control Number: 2017907804

ISBN13: 978-1-943529-94-0 paperback
        978-1-943529-95-7 eBook

Printed in the United States

Dedicated to Jacquelyn and Christopher

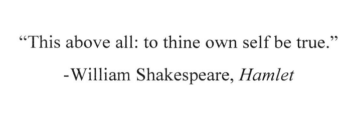

"This above all: to thine own self be true."

-William Shakespeare, *Hamlet*

# Table of Contents

Phil Jones

# Prologue


Close your eyes and imagine. Imagine you grow up with parents
or caregivers who stress hard work and a positive attitude. They
also encourage you to live by the Golden Rule, practice moral
behavior, and do the right thing. They mentor you. They inspire
you to do well in school. They praise you, when appropriate, to
build your confidence. Reasonable discipline is dispensed when
warranted. On top of this, they exhibit examples of uncon-
ditional sharing, giving, and love for family and friends. Add
another visual to this. The friends they have chosen live by the
same positive parameters and thus act as a support group.

As I write this, I am looking at a photograph from the 1950s of
my father reading from *Uncle Arthur's Bedtime Stories* to my
sister Janice (age seven) and me (age five). The contents are true
stories based on Christian values. My mother was the
photographer. This picture from one specific day could have
been shot on any day out of hundreds.

The events in this book occur between 1951 and 1962 in the
South, mainly at Hilton Head.

"The world is so full of a number of things, I'm sure we should
all be as happy as kings." -Robert Louis Stevenson

The above is one of my father's favorite quotes.

# Cocktails and Prayers

## Attitudes

The longer I live, the more I realize the importance
of choosing the right attitude in life.
Attitude is more important than facts.
It is more important than your past;
more important than your education or financial situation;
more important than your circumstances, your successes, or your failures;
more important than what other people think, say or do.
It is more important than your appearance, your giftedness, or your skills.
It will make or break a company.  It will cause a church to soar or sink.
It will make the difference between a happy home or a miserable home.
You have a choice each day regarding the attitude you will embrace.

Life is like a violin.
You can focus on the broken strings that dangle,
or you can play your life's melody on the one that remains.
You cannot change the years that have passed,
nor can you change the daily tick of the clock.
You cannot change the pace of your march toward your death.
You cannot change the decisions or the reactions of other people.
And you certainly cannot change the inevitable.
Those are the strings that dangle!
What you can do is play on the one string that remains – your attitude.
I am convinced that life is 10 percent what happens to me
and 90 percent how I react to it.
The same is true for you.

Charles R. Swindoll

The Golden Rule is generally described as "Do unto others as you would have them do unto you," which is present in the Bible and also in many, many other non-Christian religions.

Phil Jones

# Chapter One

# The *Pocahontas*

In November of 1953, my father, Dr. G. Frank Jones, Jr., purchased a double oceanfront lot on Hilton Head. The lot was number 14 in subdivision number 2, not far from the later-created roundabout known as Coligny Circle. The price of this large lot was $2,250. Before buying, he considered Pawley's Island and Kiawah. However, Hilton Head's proximity to Augusta and to his friends led Dad to purchase land there.

In 1953, a state-run car ferry began operating from Buckingham Landing, near Bluffton across Skull Creek, to Jenkins Island on the western side of Hilton Head. A one-way trip took about thirty minutes. The *Pocahontas* held nine cars and ran daily from early morning to sunset. The cost to ride was 10 cents for a pedestrian and $1.25 for a car. There were no reservations. Your arrival time determined if you made it onto the ferry.

J. Wilton Graves, a Beaufort County South Carolina state representative for whom the current bridge connecting Hilton Head to the mainland is named, was the real estate agent who sold the lot to my father. Mr. Graves then promptly scheduled the construction of the concrete block frame house. The house was architecturally designed by our next door neighbor in Augusta, Dr. William S. Boyd. Dr. Boyd, while not a trained architect, was a Renaissance man. He was a well-respected obstetrician and gynecologist. In addition, he was a talented artist (oils and water colors) and an organist, although his

3

musical talents ranked far behind his other skills. He never hesitated to entertain us with organ performances that were characterized by incessantly inharmonious chords that he quickly modulated to the correct harmonious ones by sliding his hands over the keyboard to the right or left. During the "concerts," his countenance exhibited an unwarranted self-approval that belied his displayed musical talent.

The house was architecturally functional and attractive. There was a large screened oceanside porch (twelve feet by forty-two feet, running the entire length of the home front on the upstairs level) and an approximately ninety-foot-long boardwalk, variably elevated up to seven feet, that exited the right porch and extended into the dunes close to the beach. There were three large bedrooms (front left, front right, and rear right) in addition to a large kitchen (left rear). The identically-sized, almost square bedrooms and kitchen at the four corners of the house all connected at the central large breezeway room that extended from the oceanside screened porch to the rear end (street side) of the house. Abundant sunlight and occasional moonlight were provided by the clerestory windows along the upper right side of the breezeway room. A large, crab orchard stone fireplace was placed at the front right of this big central room. Beneath this floor plan, the design included a lower level with one bedroom (front left) and a utility room (back left). The remainder of the downstairs was open space, with an indoor grill beneath the upstairs fireplace.

Soon after the lot purchase date, the house framing was accomplished. By early spring of 1954, there was a two-vehicle caravan that traveled to the unfinished Jones home every

4

Saturday until the home's completion in the early summer of 1954. In one vehicle, a cream-colored 1950 Cadillac, there was Dad, Edward Beall, and me, an eight-year-old. I served basically as a mascot. Two carpenters drove the second vehicle, a truck loaded with building supplies. We left before dawn from our Augusta home and arrived back in Augusta after dark. Mr. Beall was an excellent carpenter and a talented furniture craftsman. Handsome and around forty years old, Mr. Beall stood about 5'10" tall, weighed around 190 pounds, and had dark brown skin. His physique was that of a well-muscled athlete. He exhibited an ever-present smile and a pleasant demeanor. He was a family friend. In contrast to Mr. Beall, Dad was 6' tall with a medium complexion and brown hair. He was an attractive man.

The projects that were completed included the indoor walls and flooring. The walls were pickled pine, with different colors for each room. The flooring was predominately linoleum tile with varying colors and designs. Under close supervision, I was allowed to participate in both indoor projects.

Lunchtime on these Saturdays intrigued me. Mr. Beall's favorite lunch was pieces of fried chicken, bones still present, sandwiched between slices of white bread. He managed to eat the bread and chicken meat and leave the bones intact. Spam was the preferred choice of the other workers. Dad never ate lunch; I had a lunch-pail sandwich and a piece of fruit. This was the Saturday routine for months—leaving Augusta before daylight and arriving back after dark, making certain to catch the first morning ferry to Hilton Head and the last afternoon ferry to the mainland—until the house was completed. Upon the house's completion, Mr. Graves told Dad that it was the seventh non-native house built on Hilton Head.

Phil Jones

# Chapter Two

# Crabbing with the Westerfields—

# "It Tastes Like Chicken"

My mother, Eloise, and my father, Frank, had many friends. Two of their very best were Charles and Emily Westerfield. In 1954, during our first summer at Hilton Head, we spent time with the Westerfields. They had four sons, all athletic and handsome. Charlie was the oldest, slightly older than my sister, Janice, who would turn ten late in the summer. (I was eight.) Charlie was followed in age by Michael, George, and Cary.

On numerous occasions, both families clambered into our tan-canvas-topped red jeep, which was attached to an open gray wooden trailer, and headed out to go crabbing. The adults were in the jeep; all the kids were in the trailer. The used red jeep was bought in Augusta, Georgia, having won a 1954 beauty contest with a similarly aged green jeep. The purchase price was $250.00. Dad requested a buy-in from me of $1.00. I readily complied. My three younger brothers, ranging in age from four to less than one, stayed at the beach house with my mom. There were two tidal creeks that were both outstanding crabbing sites. One, our favorite, was at the south end of Hilton Head, 6-7 miles from home. The other was in a northern direction, 4.5 miles from home.

The latter we called "Candy's Creek" because it was in the region of her home (it is known to islanders as Folly Creek). We took a packed lunch of sandwiches, cookies, and unsweetened iced tea. The early island tap water smelled strongly of sulphur and was most unpleasant to drink. Strong, unsweetened lemon-flavored iced tea was a wonderful thirst quencher that succeeded in disguising the sulphur taste. We always drove on the deserted beach to whatever site we chose. We headed out as early as possible in the day to crab during the hours from low tide to almost high tide.

We crabbed for hours. The bait was weighted chicken necks tied to one end of a twenty-foot-long string. At the opposite end, the string was tied around a stick. The bait was tossed into the creek. When a tugging became evident, the string would be slowly wound over the stick as we worked the hungry crabs from mid-creek back to the shore. When the crabs nearly reached the shore, they would be adeptly scooped into a metal-edged rounded net attached to a broomstick-type handle. Unlike fish, crabs were always abundant and always biting. With multiple baits in the water at one time and two scoop nets, we caught hundreds of crabs during our tidal-controlled crabbing time. We always released the females and the small crabs back into the creek. The females were easily identified by the orange pouches on their undersides. If you did not lure the crabs in too fast or too jerkily, they would continue their voracious feast until they were close enough to the shore to be scooped up. A quick, smooth, deliberate net maneuver from behind the crab(s) towards the shore was almost always successful. If the scooper allowed his or her shadow to move over the crab, the crab would flee to deeper water. It was easy to feel the tugging of the baited crab. Often, there were two or three crabs working on a single chicken neck. Once netted, the crabs were placed in a container with ocean water.

We crabbed and crabbed, then ate lunch and crabbed some more. As the water approached high tide, we headed back to the house. It was always a relief to hear the engine fire up at departure time. The jeep, while usually reliable, was not uniformly so. However, it never failed us on a crabbing trip.

Back at the house, Candy cooked the crabs and, afterwards, while sitting at the dinner table, picked the meat for hours before fixing deviled crab for dinner.

The kids hit the beach at high tide for swimming before the dinner feast.

# Chapter Three

# Cocktails and Prayers

As previously stated, the beach house was completed in mid-1954, which is the first summer we stayed there.

The front screen porch on the ocean side was a favorite place to gather for conversation or reading. There was an almost constant ocean breeze. We had no air conditioning. A rope hammock stretched between vertical support beams on the left side opposite to the end with the door leading out to the boardwalk. Eight large wooden rockers with cane seats and backs were spread across the width of the porch facing the ocean.

In this inaugural summer, it was incumbent upon someone (or perhaps a team) to establish the proper foot railing height that would extend across the front side of the porch. When one sat in the rockers and stretched one's legs out horizontally, the proper foot rail height was required for optimal comfort and serenity. Doctors Westerfield and Jones, both in their early forties, assigned themselves this task. The task was believed to be too important to be turned over to underlings.

In preparation for this auspicious duty, a pitcher of Gordon Gin martinis was made and placed in the freezer. This chore would take approximately as long as the pitcher lasted. With martinis in hand, first Dr. Westerfield, then Dr. Jones, sat in a rocker and stretched his legs to a comfortable height. After alternating this practice and justifying their height selections to one another, the doctors agreed on an appropriate level for the foot railing, at least when martinis were in hand. This height was marked with a pencil, and, one morning while we were swimming, the foot railing was installed.

In the summer of 1956, we were at the beach with the Richards. Mr. Richards (Tom) was about 6', 200 pounds. He had a rugged handsomeness and an always-present mischievous twinkle in his eyes. His wife, Lillian, was a pretty 5'6", 120-pound redhead who was never surprised by Tom's larger-than-life antics. They had five lovely daughters whose ages approximated those of the five Jones kids.

One morning, after our early swim, we were hovering in the vicinity of the breakfast table when Tom, scotch in hand, stopped ten feet from the table with that ever-present mischievous look on his face, which bordered on impending glee. He released a bout of flatulence, as loud and prolonged as possible. Afterward, he had a look of self-satisfied joy. He was entertaining both himself and others. The audience tried unsuccessfully to avoid laughing. He was the "life of the party." Lillian was the kind, encouraging spouse—in my estimation, a perfect mother.

That evening, there was a prominent thunderstorm. From the breezeway, we saw an S.O.S. signal out over the ocean, probably two to three football fields from the shore. Tom swam out to the signaling boat and answered their question: "Where are we?" They had lost their bearing in the storm. He relayed the answer:

Cocktails and Prayers

"Hilton Head." (This was at a time when the Atlantic beach side of Hilton Head was almost devoid of houses and lights.)

The next morning, the weather was perfect. One adult, Dad, was there with a handful of kids. He was consistently present at the morning swim, often as the lone adult. He was our lifeguard who routinely kept up with all the children by periodically counting heads to make sure he had the "right number."

The daily cocktail parties were loud and long, starting during daylight and extending until after dark. There was lots of laughter. When Candy alerted the adults that dinner was "close" (during cocktail hours, the meaning was distinctly different for Candy than for the cocktail partiers), Mom assumed her position on the bench of the blonde Cable Nelson upright piano. She was in her early forties, 5'6", and 120 pounds. She had an attractive oval face and wavy, prematurely gray hair. George Westerfield said that she was "the whitest woman he ever met," referring to her porcelain complexion. She was an excellent pianist with strong hands and fingers, able to produce a robust sound from the piano.

First, she played a few show tunes. She always finished with "The Lord's Prayer," her signature song. This was the preamble to the sit-down prayer at the table for the adults. (The kids had, mercifully, eaten hours earlier.) Dinner was typically seafood— almost always flounder, sometimes with crab—always served with homegrown vegetables. The flounder was fresh and delicious but not recognizable as fish under the more-than-generous coating of pepper that Candy always applied.

After the late, late dinner, I feel certain there was one more prayer—this one from Candy, asking Jesus for a safe trip home.

# Chapter Four

# Thanksgiving

Every year at Thanksgiving, the G. Frank Jones family visited relatives in Tennessee. Most of the time, we stayed at my paternal grandfather's home in Jackson. We spent a smaller portion of time in Dyersburg, Tennessee, at my mother's home. These were special family times that began the same way every year.

On Wednesday morning, the day before Thanksgiving, my father performed rounds at the hospital, seeing his inpatients who would be followed during the holiday period by the on-call doctors. He arrived home late in the morning and immediately took a sleeping pill. He went upstairs to the guest bedroom, closed the door, and slept into the early evening. After an alarm awakened him, he took an "upper" to stay awake, and we piled into our 1950 cream-colored Cadillac to begin the all-night drive to Jackson. In 1954, my sister Janice was the oldest at ten years of age, followed by four brothers: an eight-year-old, a four-year-old, a two-year-old, and a one-year-old.

Edward Beal had constructed a plyboard bed with two legs that rested in the generous rear foot-well. The horizontal flat portion overrode the rear seat. The four oldest kids slept on the Edward bed, while the youngest slept up front in a bassinet which sat between my father, who drove, and my mother.

Phil Jones

The trip was punctuated with gas and bathroom stops, with one stop for coffee for my father and food for anyone who was hungry. The location was always a "fast food" place. After the coffee, food, and bathroom visits, we relocated to our berths and continued the journey. The trip started in the darkness on Wednesday night in Augusta and ended in the early morning light of Thanksgiving Day in Jackson, Tennessee.

The visiting began, fueled with adrenaline. Breakfast was served soon after our arrival: eggs, bacon, sausage (links and patties), country ham, grits, biscuits, jelly, sorghum, milk, coffee, and juices. This breakfast menu was repeated daily.

Later that day, the Thanksgiving meal was turkey with all the trimmings, followed by pies of multiple varieties and custard for dessert. My grandfather, Garland Jones, had a post-meal ritual of adding "sweetner" to his custard. The sweetener was bootleg whiskey. Ironically, he frowned on alcohol served in a glass but beamed with pleasure when "sweetening" and then eating his custard. He was basically a teetotaler, with the exception of a dose of sweetener on festive occasions.

Grandfather Jones, then in his sixties, was about 5'7" tall and around 160 pounds. He was handsome, with a full head of dark hair and an almost constant smile. Grandmother Lucille, an attractive gray-haired lady, was about the same height as Grandaddy. She was always impeccably groomed, and no one on earth was capable of being more solicitous to her children and grandchildren. We had uncles, aunts, and cousins present who made these trips the special annual events that they were. Bonnie

15

and Diane were our two pretty Tennessee cousins. Bonnie was about three years older than Janice. Diane was nine years old. During this visit, we went to the farm owned by Bonnie and Diane's parents, my dad's brother Bond and his wife Dot. Dad raced Bonnie on horseback to the barn and back, about fifty yards each way. She won easily. Later that day, the children decided to play "Hide and Seek." The barn was perfect for hiding, with plenty of hay and many compartments. The lower barn had stables and a corn crib. The loft had two large openings at each end for loading and unloading hay. A raftered rope was used by the brave to swing from the loft to the outside and jump to the ground. A manmade ladder allowed us to climb up to the loft, enter it through a small opening, and hide amongst the bales of hay or in hay tunnels. Kids from around the area routinely gathered when there was a chance to play. There was one African American youth, Bo Feet, who asked if he might participate. He was welcomed. His brothers, Poo Woo and Peanut, were not present. However, as one of the hiders, Bo Feet began to feel the pressure of finding a secure spot in the barn where he would not be found first, and hence lose. As the seeker called out loud the countdown to twenty, providing time for the hiders to hide, Bo Feet's anxiety increased. Participants heard the number, closely followed by an almost merging, significantly louder "Naw" from Bo Feet. This "Naw" crescendoed with each successive number, as did Bo Feet's apprehension. It was a merged two-syllable vocal beginning to "Hide and Seek" that was funny and entertaining to all, except to Bo Feet. It went like this: "Onenaw! TwoNAW! ThreeNAAW! FourNAAAW! FiveNAAAAW!" Finally, the "Naws" stopped. The hiders, including Bo Feet, hid. Bo Feet was not the first one found.

In between trips to the farm and visiting relatives, there was plenty of time for yard football and driveway basketball at our grandparents' home.

Early the next morning, my twenty-year-old uncle Carl, Dad, and I went quail hunting with two dogs. Dad and Carl had 12 gauge shotguns. I had a 4-10. The hunting was successful and routine, until the end. After pointing beautifully, the dogs (undoubtedly getting too close to the birds) flushed the covey prematurely. Their penalty for this was being shot at by Carl out of frustration and anger from about fifty yards away. Fortunately, the dogs were not seriously physically harmed, but, undoubtedly, they were emotionally damaged.

My grandfather did not work during these Thanksgiving visits. When he did, he was a physician, a family practitioner. He made house calls in his early career, traveling first by horse and buggy and later by car. At times, these house visits were made with some of his family alongside him. His payment ranged from nothing to a gift at Christmas—oftentimes food, such as a ham—to money from those who could afford his services. There were many times that Dr. Jones' only "payment" was knowing that he did the right thing for his fellow man.

# Chapter Five

# Marsh Tackys

In 1955, for $60, Dad purchased a gorgeous and just under 5' tall stallion for my sister Janice. She was eleven. Starlight was a chestnut Marsh Tacky with a prominent white head blaze. He was kept on Candy's pastureland, which abutted both sides of Hwy 278 (William Hilton Pkwy) and was a little over six miles from our beach house.

On a sunny summer day, Dad left Janice at Candy's to ride to our beach house. At this time, paved roadways (while present) were a scarcity, as were cars. There were widely scattered Hilton Head native houses along the route to be taken.

Two miles from Candy's, Starlight determined that he had gone far enough and balked at further travel. He was as far from his pasture as he desired to be. A kind, understanding African American family took Janice in and allowed her to tie Starlight to their porch. She determined she would wait outside for Dad to come to the rescue. Once Dad realized that Janice was late, he hopped in our red jeep along with our Hilton Head neighbor, Mr. Edwards, and traced the path between our house and Candy's. I tagged along. At first, he did this at a reasonable speed, but when he did not see Janice, his speed increased significantly as we traveled back and forth along Hwy 278. Dad cycled by Starlight and Janice two times in opposite directions before she was convinced he would not see her waving from the porch just off the road. At this point, she walked out and stood next to the road.

Dad's increasing concern and anxiety dissipated immediately when he saw his first child, obviously unharmed. If he had his surgical kit handy, he would likely have castrated Starlight on the spot. At age nine, I was given the task of riding Starlight back to Candy's under Dad's watchful eye. It was the preferred direction in Starlight's mind. There were no problems on his homeward journey; however, Starlight was on castration alert.

Within a year of this incident, we stopped at Candy's to visit her. My sister took the opportunity to run across Hwy 278 to see Starlight where he was tethered in the pasture. As she approached, Starlight ran towards her and raised up on his back hooves, brushing her forehead with a front hoof and knocking her to the ground. Dad always traveled with a sterile surgical kit. He sutured my sister's forehead with several stitches back at the beach house. Starlight was a beautiful horse that demonstrated aggressive behavior and posed a potential danger to Janice. This my father could no longer tolerate. The next time we saw Starlight, he was a gelding.

My Marsh Tacky Minnie, a filly, was purchased in 1956 when I was ten. The cost was once again $60. We went to the Squire Pope area of Hilton Head late in the day to make the transaction. Minnie was a 5' tall bay with black stocking feet. As it turned from dusk to dark, we examined Minnie. Bill Boyd, our friend and neighbor both in Hilton Head and in Augusta, mounted and rode Minnie with no saddle and no bridle. He used only a halter with an attached rope, getting Minnie to turn first one way and then the other with relative ease. When I asked him how he made this happen, he smiled and said, "It's all in the legs—that's how you get them to turn." At the same time Minnie was being evaluated, several African American men were hovering over a large fish next to an outdoor fire. One was vigorously filleting the fish, creating a bloody sight. While this side show was proceeding, Dad purchased Minnie.

Going forward, Janice and I rode together on many occasions to the beach house from Candy's, in pastures, on dirt roads, on the beach, and in the sand dunes. We usually rode bridled with Western saddles, but at times we went bareback. My favorite gait was loping, which Minnie executed beautifully for about one minute before invariably stumbling, but never falling. The missteps were disconcerting, but over time my anxiety diminished.

Not long after the purchase of Minnie, with a mixed crowd of girls and boys in attendance in Candy's pasture, I sensed the opportunity to show off in a "Watch This" moment. I stepped on a pasture stump and got astride of Minnie with only a halter and an attached rope in place. Within an instant of galloping, I suffered an immediate unanticipated dismount and flew over Minnie's head. This "Watch Me" moment turned into an immediate embarrassment because I had unbelievably forgotten that Minnie was tethered in the pasture.

Over time, the filly Minnie, aka Minnie Pearl, became a mare and had several foals, which resulted in my first business opportunity. With Candy as my partner, we split the profits.

Phil Jones

While Marsh Tackys were important to ploughing and early transportation on Hilton Head, they also provided recreation and pleasure, not to mention business opportunities.

## Chapter Six
## King of the Hill

In the 1950s, the Johannsens and the Joneses were neighbors by proximity, even though each family lived on different "streets" in Augusta, Georgia. The Johannsen brothers, Jack and Pat, lived on Woodbine Road. The Joneses resided on Laurel Lane. The Joneses' backyard abutted a neighbor of the Johannsens.

In the mid-1950s, my sister Janice and I occasionally roamed the neighborhood looking for entertainment. On one such winter afternoon, we encountered the Johannsens in their front yard. Jack and Janice, close in age, were just over ten. Pat and I, also close in age, were both under ten. We were all average-sized kids for our ages.

Realizing at this young age that defeating a neighbor in sports was rewarding, I suggested that Jack foot race Janice, but only if he wanted to lose to a girl. Cornered, he accepted and promptly lost a race that was about seventy-five feet long. Jack immediately called running a "sissy chicken" sport and challenged the Joneses to a real sport: tackle football.

He laid out the ground rules. He pointed out the side bounds and the goal lines. Their front yard was roughly seventy-five by seventy-five feet. Each team had four downs to go from one goal line to the other. The first team to score four touchdowns won. If the team who had the ball first reached four touchdowns, the other team was given an opportunity to tie up the score. There was no traditional coin toss. Jack said that it was their yard, so they got the ball first.

Both offenses were unstoppable. Jack and Janice were the star running backs. Pat and I were the under-appreciated centers. Neither offensive team was close to being thwarted. All offensive plays were runs. On average, three plays were required for each team to negotiate the field. There were no fumbles. In short order, the Johannsens reached four scores. The Joneses tied with their fourth touchdown minutes later.

Without prompting or encouragement, I summarized the athletic events of the afternoon for Jack and Pat. The Joneses were undefeated (one win, one tie), while the Johannsens had one loss and were lucky to tie in football. Jack assured me the race did not count. He reiterated it was a "sissy chicken" sport. Fortunately, or unfortunately, this was a one-off event.

# Chapter Seven

# The Bridge

There are two explanations for the population of Hilton Head changing from 300 in 1950 to 37,099 (from census data) in 2010. These reasons both occurred in the 1950s. In 1950, the first electricity was brought to the island. This was an extremely important lifestyle improvement. The second reason was the James F. Byrnes two-lane swing bridge, which was constructed and completed in 1956. (James F. Byrnes was a South Carolinian who was elected governor in addition to holding several other political positions.) The round-trip toll was $2.50.

Both of these fueled Hilton Head to become what it is today. Before the bridge, living off the land was a mainstay—i.e. hunting, fishing, and farming. When there was more than the family needed, one could contract with Mr. Charles Simmons, Sr., aka "Mr. Transportation," to carry the excess goods via boat to Savannah to be sold in the Farmer's Market. There was also a much, much smaller market of non-native island inhabitants in the 1950s before the bridge was completed. An example of this occurred at our beach house when a middle-aged African American drove to our home in a dull black 1950ish Ford panel truck with a dusty patina, stopped, and robustly sang from the adjacent street, "Vegetable and Shrimp Man." It sounded like "VegeTOBull and Shrimp (this word was crescendoed to a higher pitch) Man." This sung phrase was always the same on the many occasions he came by our house. It intrigued me, I liked hearing it, and I still can hear it to this day. We always bought both vegetables and shrimp. They were fresh and delicious.

When the swing bridge was completed, the initial traffic was modest, allowing northwest islanders to literally count the arriving cars as they made a signature sound over the metal portion of the bridge. The pattern of life gradually changed from living off the land to obtaining a job, perhaps related to the plantations that were being developed, or to starting a business. In 1956, the Richardsons opened the first supermarket on the island. Instead of islanders going out the back door and wringing a chicken's neck for dinner, they began to go to the store where they might purchase a chicken.

On the island, transportation before the bridge was often riding bareback on a Marsh Tacky with a halter and a rope. After the bridge, cars became more plentiful, and Marsh Tacky travel diminished. I asked two male native islanders, "Was life on Hilton Head better before or after the bridge?" Their answers, without hesitation, were identical. It was better after the bridge because of the job opportunities that were created.

# Chapter Eight

# Baseball, Prayers, and as Good as New

Nancy Ford, whom we called "Candy," lived just over six miles from our Hilton Head home in North Forest Beach. Her grandson, Arthur, lived with her. Her home faced Hwy 278, the William Hilton Parkway. The front yard variably served as farmland for growing produce and pastureland where horses were tied. There was no fencing. The area was roughly two-hundred feet wide by two-hundred feet long. Hwy 278 formed the east border of her property. Behind the home on the western side was Broad Creek. The parcel of land between the house and the road served another important purpose. It was a baseball field.

On this particular day, there were four baseball players. Arthur, called Pete by some, was one of the players, as was his teenage cousin Clarence. My father, G. Frank Jones, a general surgeon in Augusta, Georgia, was the third participant. I was the fourth. Dad was forty-three, Arthur was twelve, and I was ten. There were only two bases, home plate and first base. There were two fielders, a pitcher who was also the infielder, and the outfielder. Once the right and left field foul lines were established, the game began.

From the time we first met, Arthur and I were fast friends. We were always teammates. We were underdogs, but that didn't matter. We were playing baseball on a beautiful day. Clarence was the best of all of us. He could hit the ball over the parkway.

Dad was a consistent "hit 'em where they ain't" batter who always hit the ball far away from where the outfielder was stationed. Arthur and I had no hitting power and no strategy, but we loved to play. The older guys were up first. After they scored numerous runs, we finally got them out and were ready to bat. Dad pitched. Clarence was in the outfield. Arthur batted first. We had only his one at bat, a grounder to the pitcher, which resulted in a foot race to first base. A tag to the back propelled Arthur to fall forward with outstretched hands to dampen his fall. Dad helped Arthur up and immediately realized he had a right forearm fracture that did not break through the skin. During the process of lifting a crying, obviously in pain Arthur to his feet, Dad set the fracture and held on to Arthur's forearm.

While Dad securely held Arthur's forearm, I drove the jeep back to our beach house. Candy, our cook, noticed us pulling into the driveway earlier than expected. She looked out the Miami window in the breezeway room and realized something was wrong. Rushing out the door to meet us, she began sobbing in concert with Arthur and repeatedly saying, "Oh Jesus! Oh Jesus! Oh Jesus!" This prayerful supplication was comforted and softly answered by my father, who assured Candy that the fracture was set and that it would heal "as good as new." While Candy stood next to Dad, it was obvious that she was about his age and his height but weighed slightly more. Her beautiful ebony skin and black hair complimented her characteristic smile. Now, that smile was replaced by anguish and sobbing. As emotions subsided, Dad got Candy to hold the forearm while he searched for the material needed to splint the fracture in a cast. Pieces of plyboard and adhesive tape were applied, followed by a final outside wrapping with Ace bandages. Dad explained to Candy to keep the cast on until he removed it in about two months. He told her to keep it dry.

At the time, I did not think Candy's outcry of "Oh Jesus!" was a prayer, for it was so different from the ones that I had previously heard, but it clearly was. In contrast, the Joneses' mealtime and nighttime prayers, as we said them while growing up, are listed below. In addition, I am including three other special prayers.

### Jones Children Mealtime Prayer

God is Great,
God is Good,
Let us thank Him for our food.
By His hands we all are fed,
Give us Lord our Daily Bread.
Amen

### Jones Children Nighttime Prayer

Lord I thank Thee for the way
That Thou hast led me all the day.
Oh Savior keep me through the night
That I may see the morning light,
And from my heart all evil take.
All this I ask for Jesus' sake.
Amen

This was a comforting nightly routine.

Phil Jones

## The Serenity Prayer

God, grant me the serenity
to accept the things I cannot change;
courage to change the things I can;
and the wisdom to know the difference.
-Reinhold Niebuhr

The entire Serenity Prayer is actually longer. The part above is the most recognized. It is the AA prayer. To me, it can be summed up, although much less elegantly: "Make the best of any situation."

## Prayer of Saint Francis of Assisi for Peace

Lord, make me an instrument of Your peace,
Where there is hatred, let me sow love.
Where there is injury, let me sow pardon.
Where there is friction, let me sow union.
Where there is error, let me sow truth.
Where there is doubt, let me sow faith.
Where there is despair, let me sow hope.
Where there is darkness, let me sow light.
Where there is sadness, let me sow joy.
O Divine Master,
Grant that I may not so much seek to be consoled as to console,
to be understood as to understand, to be loved as to love.
For it is in giving that we receive.
It is in pardoning that we are pardoned.
It is in dying that we are born to eternal life. Amen.

The ultimate prayer of doing the right thing.

Give us grace and strength to forbear and to persevere. Give us courage and gaiety, and the quiet mind. Spare to us our friends, soften to us our enemies. Bless us, if it may be, in all our innocent endeavors. If it may not, give us strength to encounter that which is to come, that we may be brave in peril, constant in tribulation, temperate in wrath, and in all changes of fortune, and down to the gates of death, loyal and loving to one another.

-Robert Louis Stevenson

This is a beautiful prayer that is a mixture of asking for help and encouragement to do the right thing.

As regards "As Good as New," Arthur's fracture healed beautifully. He was treated instantly and compassionately. He never had an x-ray, hospital or office visit, or a plaster cast. All these things were unavailable on Hilton Head in the mid-1950s when the fracture occurred.

# Chapter Nine

# Barkey

In the late summer of 1956, the five Jones children ranged in age from twelve to two. We were spending a week at Hilton Head with our aunt Chi Cha and her six kids. Their age spread was similar to ours, only slightly younger. "Chi Cha" was our attempt to say "Sister," my dad's name for his sibling. George, the McInnes patriarch, joined us at the end of his general surgical work week to spend the last two nights of the summer vacation with us. We called him "Uncle Mac."

Bill and Willets Boyd, our Augusta and Hilton Head neighbors, were also on the island. As young children, we struggled with the name "Elizabeth," so it permanently became "Willets."

Bill, as stated earlier, was a Renaissance man. Having no children allowed him to have the time for multiple talents and avocations to blossom. He had a red and white single propeller airplane that transported the Boyds from Augusta to Hilton Head. His private airport was the Hilton Head Beach, which in 1956 was largely deserted (the swing bridge opened in 1956). Like my mom, Bill was fair-skinned and spent very little time on the beach. Most of his beach activity included taking off and landing. The Jones children were still young enough to be charming and endearing. We were forbidden by dad to fly, although permission to taxi up and down the beach was granted.

Barkey was named by the kids for the obvious reason. He was a handsome young fawn boxer in 1956. In Augusta, he and the children were enclosed in a backyard bordered by a five-foot-high cyclone fence. Scattered around the backyard were several playground equipment items—a merry-go-round, a swing set, a slide, and a jungle gym. As kids in Augusta, we spent hour after hour playing in the backyard. Barkey was there, enriching our childhood with his participation. He learned to climb the fence, but there was no motivation to escape because his playmates were all inside. He entertained us by taking turns on the slide, which was elevated five feet off the ground. He was an integral part of our family.

The last night of our stay on Hilton Head was memorable. Uncle Mac, on the first of these two nights, told me repeatedly of the beauty of sex and love. They were both mysteries to a ten-year-old male, but my curiosity was peaked. I wanted to learn more. A lot more. On the last night of our vacation, the Jones and McInnes kids were bedded on the front oceanside screened-in porch while Mom, Dad, Uncle Mac, and Aunt Chi Cha ate dinner thirty feet away. As kids are wont to do, we chattered and laughed in the time before falling asleep.

Suddenly, there was a screaming male voice in our midst. It was Uncle Mac literally threatening the elder children if we did not allow the younger children to go to sleep. This tirade went on for several minutes before he returned to dinner. Not an additional word was uttered by the frightened porch audience.

On the day of our departure, while Bill Boyd was taxiing for take-off, Barkey was hit by the airplane propeller. He was unconscious and bleeding profusely from his head.

It was at this point that Uncle Mac took charge. He wrapped Barkey's head in towels and put pressure on the hemorrhaging wound. From that point forward, he sat in the back seat of our car, holding Barkey's wrapped head in his lap until hours later when we arrived back in Augusta. He took Barkey to his office and operated that night. Several days later, our pet was in the backyard playing as if nothing had happened.

Within a twenty-four-hour period, my impression of an angry, mean-spirited person was challenged by this heroic, selfless act to save a dog's life.

# Chapter Ten

# Erosion

In the mid-1950s, those who looked for a snapshot of erosion could easily find it. The sandy shore located a mile north of the current circle at Coligny Plaza had numerous tree stumps rising from the beach sand.

Property owners in the North Forest Beach area saw how destructive beach erosion could be over time. Well over a hundred feet of oceanfront land disappeared where erosion was most prominent.

High tides, which occur two times every day, were responsible for this dune loss. The tides are caused by a gravitational pull from the moon and the sun. When the moon and sun are aligned this results in higher tides (called spring tides), which are unrelated to any season. When nor'easters impact upon high tides, the erosion is accelerated. Hurricanes have the potential for extreme erosion.

This erosion concentrated in the northern Atlantic beaches of Hilton Head led many land owners to choose to build rock seawalls along the coast. This expensive process was paid for by individual property owners. With the passage of time, these seawalls, once extremely obvious, have been essentially buried beneath sand.

(Several beach re-nourishments have taken place along a six to seven-mile front between Port Royal Plantation and an area just south of Coligny Circle. These are very large, expensive projects funded by the town of Hilton Head. In essence, sand is pumped from the ocean floor through pipeline and deposited on the beach.)

The consequences of erosion produced angst in oceanfront homeowners in the affected areas until it was addressed initially by seawalls and later by beach re-nourishment. It's likely that those who bought property in the 1950s and later, under duress put up seawalls to protect their property's integrity, spent more money on the seawall than on the combined investment of the land and the house.

While erosion has resulted in significant property loss and owner consternation, it is easy to overlook for the occasional visitor to Hilton Head. However, those who have taken a walk, jog, or bike ride at high tide have discovered that there are areas where the ocean at high tide is far from the sand dunes and other sites where the incoming waves crash into the dunes. Body surfers in areas of erosion after seawalls were built learned quickly to end their wave ride before crashing headfirst into dangerous rocks.

# Chapter Eleven

# "Where's Dennis?"

It was late in the summer of 1957. The Jones clan was returning from their Hilton Head, South Carolina home to Augusta, Georgia. There were seven of us in the big white 1955 Chrysler station wagon. Daddy—Frank, G. Frank, or Dr. Jones, depending on the conversant—was driving. Mother, Eloise, was at his side. They were in their early forties. All the trip stuff sat in the back. Lots of stuff. Amongst the stuff sat their five offspring, ranging in age from thirteen to just under four. Janice, my sister, was the eldest, followed by four almost-evenly-spaced boys.

There were no seat belts and no car seats for children. Most of the time, all five kids were in the back two seats. Occasionally, a favorite would work his way into the front middle. A favorite always came from the youngest three. The wagon was big and had three rows of seats only because there wasn't a bigger version with more rows of seats.

The parental decibel tolerance was usually approached and more often exceeded by one-third to one-half of the way to Augusta. This time, the stopping point was Ridgeland, South Carolina. There were several routes that could be taken between Hilton Head and Augusta, none of them good. They all frequently traversed small towns, requiring a slowing down from the highway speed of 55 mph.

When we stopped at a Gulf Station with two separate gasoline tanks (regular and high test) in Ridgeland, almost immediately, an employee would come up to the driver's window. My father always said, "Fill 'er up, high test, and please check the oil." "Yes, sir," always followed. Without my father asking, the front windshield was also cleaned.

We then proceeded to fall out, go to the restroom, and drink some water. There never was a time when we were offered soft drinks, crackers, candies, or any type of food. We knew not to ask. There was a "Whites Only" sign over two restrooms—one men, one women. A "Colored" sign marked a third. Similarly, there was a "Whites Only" water fountain and a second designated "Colored." After we used the restroom and got water and my father paid the few dollars he owed in cash (there were no credit or debit cards), we resumed our positions in the wagon. There was never a roll call. When things felt right—i.e. the decibel level was at the usual for trip resumption—the big white Chrysler would be ignited, and off we would go.

On this occasion, about fifteen minutes onward to Augusta, it was determined that we were one Jones short. Why this occurred, I don't know, but I suspect it was one of the three older little geniuses who blurted out, "Where's Dennis?"

I have often wondered if this was an attempt to "thin the herd." Five kids are an overabundance of good fortune, and as time passed I realized there were only two or maybe three of us worth keeping. However, the "thin the herd" conspiracy does not hold water in this instance—Dennis was too special. Now, if it had been any of the other four left in Ridgeland, the conspiracy would have been warranted.

I have even speculated on Dennis's career path had he become a Ridgelander. Over the years, there was encouragement from my father for the males to pursue a career in medicine, i.e. follow his path and become a physician. This push was variably fervent, as determined by the perceived stubbornness of the particular child. Absent this parental push, growing up in Ridgeland, Dennis would have become head of the town council, later Mayor, then onward to Governor of South Carolina before assuming the United States presidency. In the Ronald Reagan mode, he would have been a great president with a magnificent sense of humor.

Phil Jones

# Chapter Twelve

# High Tide

Ideally, every child experiences special days. For me, they were Christmas Eve, Christmas, my birthday, and high tide days at the beach with family and friends.

On a typical summer day at the beach in the mid-1950s, the Westerfield and the Jones children (ranging in age from teenagers to children less than three) awakened to the sunrise over the Atlantic Ocean. The children older than the very youngest all slept on the screened eastern oceanside porch that extended the width of the house. We slept on a mixture of army cots and pallets on the floor. A hammock at one end of the porch provided an additional bed.

Before we could go swimming, we had chores that required minutes, not hours, to accomplish. (Mom and Dad felt like daily chores were important, even on vacation.) We folded sheets and stored cots and pallets in an orderly area on the back wall of the porch. On some days, we swept.

With chores out of the way, we raced down the boardwalk to the beach, not stopping for any reason until we had reached an ocean depth of above waist high, where we could no longer run or even move with any speed. Dad was not far behind. On the way to this above-waist-high point, we ran through incoming waves if they were manageable, jumped some, and ducked under the most powerful ones. It was at this point that we stopped and evaluated where the waves were breaking. Usually they were perfect in this area, or out slightly further, for body surfing. We had a few five-foot-long canvas rafts that were used by the youngest. The most exhilarating fun was body surfing. If you caught a wave just right (at its point of breaking over), the stopping point was when your front side abraded against the sand on the beach. Then you whooped to anyone who would listen, "Did you see that?" We did not stop riding waves until about two hours later when we were summoned by an adult vigorously ringing a brass bell hanging from the eave next to the porch screen door, assisted in this "Come in to eat" by a second adult at the end of the boardwalk, whose waving arm motioned us towards the house. Reluctantly, we headed in, stopping at the boardwalk shower to rinse off and towel dry before entering the house. There were no shoes or sandals. There was never any sunscreen, lip screen, hats, caps, or sunglasses used on the beach. We sat on one of the four small benches around the rectangular table at the edge of the kitchen. Each bench easily accommodated two bigger kids or three smaller kids. One narrow end of this table was attached to the wall. At the other end, there was room for a chair or two. Candy had a beaming smile as we exchanged "Good mornings" while she brought eggs, bacon, sausage, grits, tomatoes, biscuits, and gravy to the table. (A typical breakfast on the rare days when Candy was not present was oatmeal with butter and brown sugar.) Milk and orange juice were the beverage options. We all had a "good hearty," as my paternal grandfather would say, describing a voracious appetite. Our breakfast discussions were jubilant, predominately related to how good we were at riding waves. There was never modesty or understatement. Overstatement and braggadocio were utilized nonstop with anyone who would listen. We knew that after eating there would be a mandatory one-hour rest period before we were allowed to go back to the beach. We were encouraged to make effective use of this time by reading. We did so, with George Westerfield setting the best example by being the first to open and the last to close a book before heading back to the beach. During our vacation times, he was by far the best reader. On a very rare occasion, my father would take this rest period to read to us. On one such time, he read the entire first chapter of Genesis and the first two verses of the second chapter. He took this opportunity to explain that these huge creations that occurred in six days may have taken a lot longer. As he explained it, a day at that time could have been one thousand years or even thousands of years. My take as a ten-year-old optimist was that God could do anything. He probably didn't even need six days for the major accomplishments described.

# Chapter Thirteen

# Low Tide

Activities at low tide were fun, too. Lots of fun. Depending on the number of participants, there was either a softball game on the beach or roll to the bat. The latter game could occur with a minimum of two participants. The batter tossed the ball vertically to himself and hit the ball toward the ocean to an outfielder or outfielders. If the ball was caught in the air by the fielder, the batter and fielder exchanged places. A fielded ground ball was rolled to the bat that was placed parallel to the shoreline. The wind was a variable that had to be taken into consideration before the ball was rolled. If the wind was significant, the ball would break or curve with the wind, just as a golf putt would. If the ball hit the bat with sufficient speed, the ball would bounce up, allowing the batter to catch it. If the ball was caught, all positions remained unchanged. If the ball slowly died at the bat, it would not rebound to be caught, and the roller and batter then changed positions.

"Tag" was a standard game whereby there was an "it" individual trying to chase down and tag others. Once tagged by the "it" person, the tagged person became "it," and the tagger joined the group trying to avoid being tagged. Usually there was a base (e.g. a towel on the beach) involved that allowed one immunity from becoming "it." My variation of tag, which I called "Moving Base," was more fun and required more skill. In this game, a tennis ball was the base, and when the "non-it" perceived the tagger getting close to an individual, the tennis ball was thrown to the imperiled person, thereby providing base protection. This added a touch of frustration to being "it" and enhanced the fun. At the more advanced level of "Moving Base," one could require left hand throws and catches only, or the ball had to bounce once before being caught. "Moving Base" helped participants enhance the cynical element of their personalities if it needed encouraging.

The adults came up with a different form of low tide entertainment. This was analogous to skiing but required significantly less skill. A rope was attached to the back of the jeep and to a square piece of plyboard. A second rope of a similar length was also attached to the jeep and held by a kid who sat on the board and was pulled along the beach.

My father was inspired by his good friend Tom Richards, and after Tom bought a Sunfish sailboat, Dad was moved to follow suit. Safety first. In the late 1950s, the lovely Richards daughters taught my sister Janice and me to sail at Clarks Hill Lake. They stressed the importance of not sailing into electrical wires because the result could be deadly.

With the instruction completed, Dad bought a small sailboat and trailer in Allendale, South Carolina on the way to Hilton Head. This was a boat with a single sail, about fifteen-foot-long and a few feet wide. After we assured Dad that we were sufficiently knowledgeable about sailing, he allowed us to enter the ocean but made us promise to stay close to shore. On that inaugural voyage that started in front of our beach house and headed north in the direction of Port Royal Sound, my sister and I sailed beautifully. Dad ran parallel to us on the shore for about one hundred yards, prepared to save us if needed, before he became convinced that all was well. We sailed many times after the initial voyage, continually progressing further away from shore.

A nighttime beach adventure was shared with the Westerfields. One summer, with a moonlit ocean, the kids were awakened in what seemed like the middle of the night and took their places in the trailer behind the jeep. The adults rode in the jeep. We headed south and within minutes spotted a loggerhead turtle's typical tire track marking on the sand that led to its nest.

We went to the nest and gently uncovered it, and each kid who desired held a ping pong-sized, leathery-feeling egg. We then replaced the egg, re-covered the nest, and returned home to finish our interrupted night's sleep.

While most of the Hilton Head events were just fun things, occasionally, the fun was mixed with education. The adults stressed the importance of extinguishing the outdoor lights between May and November because this was nesting time. Both the adult female turtles and the hatchlings rely on moonlight reflecting off the ocean to guide them back to the ocean. The adults said that outdoor lights competed with nature's moonlight and confused both the female and the hatchlings. We were very lucky to have parents (the Westerfields and the Joneses) who wanted us to learn, to enjoy adventures, and, above all, to become good stewards of the earth.

Phil Jones

# Chapter Fourteen

# The Monkeys

In the early 1950s, the infectious disease poliomyelitis was an ever-present fear of parents. While most polio virus infections were asymptomatic, in rare cases, they resulted in weakness, paralysis, and even death. President Franklin Roosevelt's paralysis was likely due to polio. The Salk vaccine, which was licensed in 1955, was an injectable dose of inactivated virus. (The Sabin vaccine utilized an attenuated polio virus. It was given orally and was licensed in 1962.) These two vaccines largely eradicated polio around the world.

The Salk vaccine employed monkey tissue culture. A monkey farm, such as the old monkey farm in the Pinckney Colony on the mainland close to Hilton Head, was often reported to be instrumental in the polio vaccine development. The Rhesus monkey not only was of critical importance to the Salk vaccine development, but it also was used in other vaccine creations and other forms of medical research.

When I was an eight-year-old, I did not consider the research angle of the Rhesus monkeys when we periodically went to the cemetery at the corner of Mathews Drive and William Hilton Parkway to observe the monkeys. This cemetery had numerous grave sites that dated back to the 18th century and included Revolutionary War participants. The monkeys did not typically exhibit the bared teeth expression, grooming of a peer, or rump exposure so often seen with zoo monkeys. They seemed as fascinated to study us as we did them. They periodically interrupted their human examinations to demonstrate tree gymnastics. We observed monkeys in the 1950s. When the swing bridge was completed in 1956, this coincided with the beginning of the rapid extinction of the Hilton Head monkeys. While we saw the monkeys only in the cemetery area, at least one ventured beyond its confines onto a farm. When the farmer discovered the monkey stealing corn from a horse trough, he shot and killed it. There is an AP wirephoto in *The Augusta Chronicle* of Dr. W.E. Hoy, head of the University of South Carolina Biology Department, holding this dead monkey, dated April 10, 1958. Two weeks after the wirephoto, there was a follow-up article. In this, the name Henry H. McKeithan, a USC senior, is mentioned. I personally communicated with Mr. McKeithan on September 6, 2015 and September 7, 2015 to discuss this event. Mr. McKeithan stated that he and Dr. Hoy picked up the monkey the day after it was shot and took it back to the University of South Carolina for further study. (The Rhesus monkey was identical to the type used for polio vaccine development and other medical research.) Mr. McKeithan said that they did not think that the Hilton Head monkey tribe was native to the island. Dr. Hoy postulated a nearby shipwreck with the monkeys swimming to shore as a possible origin of the Hilton Head tribe.

Phil Jones

# Chapter Fifteen

# The Cola Tasting

One summer in the early 1960s, my sister Janice, our cousin Diane, and I were all teenagers. Diane and I were in the mid-teens, and Janice was a little older. We were at Hilton Head. Dad worked in Augusta four days a week (Monday - Thursday) and spent three full days (Friday - Sunday) at Hilton Head. He would leave the island long before dawn on Monday morning and return after dark on Thursday. This work pattern was invariable, which allowed us to plan the Cola tasting in his absence. His absence was required for the project to go forward. My sister Janice took charge of the arrangements. When Dad was absent, Mom would drive Candy home after dinner. We knew we had at least forty minutes of tasting and perhaps sixty if Mom and Candy sat and talked before Candy went into her home. On the morning of this fateful day, Janice purchased a fifth of white rum. She was and looked several years beneath the legal drinking age. Anyhow, the purchase was successful, and as Mom was backing out of the driveway on the street side, the three tasters were racing to the end of the boardwalk next to the beach on the opposite side of the house. We quickly mixed three drinks of rum and cola and commenced with the speed tasting. The experience, at least early on, was refreshing. My profanity spigot was wide open. Up to this point, I had never used profanity. Mom stressed that it was "poverty of speech"; however, on this night, I was able to fold both "damn" and "hell" at least once into every alcohol-laced, sagacious sentence. Because of the time constraints, this task was pursued at an accelerated rate. We knew the project must be completed before Mom walked in the house. We almost pulled it off to perfection.

We were all back in the house when Mom returned. I immediately began vomiting. Mom asked, "What's wrong?" Janice said I had an upset stomach from dinner, but the vomitus betrayed us because it reeked of rum. Mom needed less than an instant to analyze and diagnose.

We all slept it off and did not ever repeat the Cola tasting. I am sure Mom told Dad the story when he arrived back at Hilton Head. He never mentioned it. Appropriately measured discipline was a tenet of Jones parenting; however, in this case, my parents must have felt we had been adequately punished.

Phil Jones

# Chapter Sixteen

# The Chlorophyll Golf Ball

My father loved golf. More accurately, he really, really loved golf. He practiced general surgery in Augusta, Georgia—on many days going to work before sunup and returning home after sunset. On these long days, when he arrived home, he stepped outside the kitchen entrance to an area lit by a security light. There, he swung a club over and over again, feeling the swing, the posture, the stance, and the leather grip, so he would be ready to perform at his best when he was rewarded with both daylight and an available son or sons to accompany him to the golf course.

He was a Ben Hogan disciple, and, when circumstances allowed, he walked close to Ben's side, up and down the fairways of the Augusta National Golf Course. In the early Masters Tournament days, patrons were not roped away from the players as they are today. Ben probably wondered, "Who is this guy that shadows me for hours? I hope he's undercover security. He's way too close." When Dad got home, he discussed with his sons the beauty of Ben's beautiful grass divots, so long and so deep. Incidentally, in the beginning years of the Masters, there were individuals armed with tickets walking in downtown Augusta, giving them to anyone who would go. In those days, the patron audience was sparse compared to later when a ticket became difficult, and then almost impossible, to obtain.

Cocktails and Prayers

My father, in spite of his love for golf, never got help for his smothered low hook, an ugly shot that traveled low, left, and short of the intended target. This shot haunted him throughout his golfing career, as did his sons' golf shots when they took up golf at an early age.

When the George Cobb-designed Ocean Course was built in Sea Pines in 1960, Dad became a charter member. It took but one round on the back nine of the course (which opened first) for Dad to realize that the lagoons were a magnet for Jones-struck golf balls. The next time we played on Hilton Head, Dad provided us with golf balls with the word "Topace" written on them. The advantage that Dad sought was that they floated on top of the lagoon water and hence were retrievable. He felt this far outweighed the disadvantage that his sons noticed, which was that when the ball was struck semi-solidly, the initial round shape morphed into an ovoid "egg" one. While this undoubtedly saved Dad a small fortune in golf balls, the Jones kids never recovered from the stigmata of his obvious lack of trust in their ball striking abilities. It's also decidedly harder to make putts with an egg-shaped golf ball.

In 1962, Dad experienced his "every dog has his day" golf round, with me alongside. We were playing the front nine of the Ocean Course in Sea Pines and stopped on the 7th tee to let two young (early twenties) men go through. Dad and I watched intently as the first young man addressed his ball and hit a beautiful shot that stopped right next to the pin on the 170 yard par 3, a certain birdie. The second then addressed his ball and hit it as far right of the green as humanly possible, deep into the woods. Without any utterance or hesitation, this second golfer placed his golf club below his knee, with the grip in his left hand and the shaft next to the clubhead in his right hand, and snapped the club into two pieces. He then placed the severed club in the trash container, got in the golf cart with his playing partner, and drove away towards the green.

That day I learned a valuable lesson: *Don't let a golf club that disrespects you get away with it. The other clubs are looking— you need to set an example.* I also was reminded of one of Dad's favorite sayings: "Whom the gods would destroy, they first make angry." (This is undoubtedly derived from the quote "Whom the gods would destroy, they first make mad," spoken by Prometheus in Henry Wadsworth Longfellow's poem "The Masque of Pandora" (1875).)

Dad and I finished the round. It was his only time in his life to shoot in the 30s for 9 holes. His final score was 39. He hit a driver and then a 3 or 5 wood to all five par 4s, hitting onto or next to all the greens. His play on the two par 3s and two par 5s was also much better than I had ever seen.

His 39 placed him in a higher-than-a-kite mood. It was a great experience to share his best scoring day with him.

In spite of his love of the game, he was usually a fairly awful golfer. He told me that if he played really well, his patients would wonder if he was spending too much time on the course and not enough time honing his surgical skills in the operating room. Almost everyone knew he was an awful golfer. Almost everyone knew he was a skilled surgeon with an excellent bedside manner.

Every Christmas in Augusta, there were two rooms for gifts: the playroom for the kids' presents and the den for the adult gifts. Mr. Bill Watkins, a patient and a friend, gave gag gifts to Dad every year. Dad received the chlorophyll golf ball on Christmas Day in 1961, the year before he was to shoot his one and only 9 hole round in the 30s. The golf ball was chlorophyll green and was centered in a beautiful mahogany plaque with a caption beneath the ball: The Chlorophyll Golf Ball for the Stinking Golfer.

## Chapter Seventeen

## The Physician's Physician

World War II, the deadliest war in history, occurred between 1939 and 1945. Civilian and military assignments were coordinated. While many eligible physicians were conscripted into military service, a rare individual was designated for a civilian position. The latter was the case for my father who, in 1944, at age thirty-one, became the Acting Head of the Department of Surgery at the Medical College of Georgia. He held this position until 1946.

His practice in general surgery expanded rapidly because of his reputation as a skilled surgeon with a winning bedside manner.

When in Augusta, he worked long hours. A respite was provided after the Hilton Head home was built in 1954. There was no phone in our beach house for decades, something Dad really liked.

Dad had multiple traits that served him well, mainly discipline, determination to succeed, and attitude. He was meticulously conscientious. If he was to perform an operation, undertake a project, or start an exercise program, he would do it to the best of his ability. In short, he had all the traits you would want your surgeon to have.

As regards physician's physician, if a doctor or doctor's family needed a general surgeon, Dr. Jones was high in demand because of his surgical skills and bedside manner, as previously mentioned.

He began running in his forties and continued a daily rigorous physical training (PT) program for the remainder of his life. He especially loved jogging. When he ran towards you on the beach, you would recognize his signature arm movements from quite a distance, long before his facial features were discernible. His left arm was almost stationary, while his right arm moved in a unique circular motion. After his PT regimen was established, he added a nutritional component. This included two tablespoons of wheat bran on top of his morning cereal, euphemistically designated as "dynamite" by his sons.

As busy as he was, he reserved time for his children. Friday night was "surprising," which was always a drive-in cowboy movie at the Skyview in Augusta. As we grew older, we enjoyed a golf trip to Highlands, North Carolina. In the spring of 1962, Dad took me on one such trip. I was sixteen. I was the family favorite (perhaps an exaggeration, Top Five favorite is more accurate). The golf, while forgettable, was punctuated by a life experience worth relating. As we finished the 9th hole, which has a lodge in the backdrop, I noticed a statuesque beauty standing at the window, as if interested in watching golf. She was a few years older than I was. I admire anyone who will seek out incredible golf, but the fact that she was nude, staring, and seemingly not interested in moving or covering up made her even more alluring. It's not common that you see beautiful female breasts in a golf round, but it does happen periodically.

# Epilogue

We called her "Candy." Her family called her "Candy Doll" because, as her granddaughter Brenda Williams wrote, "She is and was 'so sweet.'"

Nancy Ford— "Candy" to the Joneses, "Candy Doll" to others— was a special person. When first meeting her, you would be impressed by her Gullah language. It wouldn't take long to realize that behind those beautiful words was a person of unique kindness and wisdom, a person from whom you could learn. A person from whom you wanted to learn. A person whose thoughts you wanted to hear and with whom you wanted to share your own thoughts.

Candy Doll's church, Queen Chapel African Methodist Episcopal Church, is on Hilton Head, South Carolina. This church celebrated its 150th anniversary in 2015. It is the second oldest church on the island.

Brenda Williams contacted me in July 2015 and asked if I would be interested in writing something for the souvenir journal. I thanked her for asking me and said, "Yes, I would be honored." I wrote the following on July 20, 2015 and submitted it for inclusion in the journal.

Candy Doll Ford

Cocktails and Prayers

The Frank Jones family met Candy Doll Ford in 1954 on Hilton Head Island, South Carolina. She immediately became an integral part of our family. Her regal bearing was never without a smile. Her attitude was a lesson for all. Her inspiration and love of Jesus were limitless. She loved her family boundlessly. She blessed the five Jones kids with her wisdom, encouragement, and kindness. She loved to sing, and on occasion would ask my sister, Janice, to play "Jesus Keep Me Near the Cross" which she sang beautifully like an angel of God. She taught us how to cook. She taught us how to live. We love you, Candy Doll.

Phil and Julie Jones

Phil Jones

# Acknowledgements

HENRY DRIESSEN, who welcomed me into his home and patiently shared insights into the changes of Hilton Head from the pre-bridge era to the post-bridge era.

JANICE HITCHCOCK, WAYNE JONES, DENNIS JONES, and VERNON JONES, siblings who were the stars in this story. Thanks for sharing and helping me remember these long-ago events.

DIANE FRADELLA, cousin supreme and star on equal footing with my siblings. Thanks for sharing and helping me remember these long-ago events.

GEORGE AND MICHAEL WESTERFIELD, family friends, participants in the story who aided and enhanced my memory of these long-ago events.

DR. HAROLD S. ENGLER, Dad's surgical partner, Dad's good friend, and a physician's physician.

MERN (Marion) ATWATER, one of the lovely Richards daughters who aided and enhanced my memory of these long-ago events.

57

ARTHUR BURKE, Candy's adored grandson and my friend who filled important gaps in the story.

BRENDA WILLIAMS, Candy's loving granddaughter who filled important gaps in the story.

PHIL BROWN, friend since grammar school who found Henry H. McKeithan expeditiously for me after I had failed.

HENRY H. McKEITHAN, who patiently discussed and educated me on more than one occasion regarding my obsession with the monkeys.

JULIE, my wife and proofreader who discovered my mother's treasure trove of newspaper clippings about Hilton Head from the 1950s and 1960s.

JACQUELYN WHETZEL, my daughter, my proofreader, and my initial manuscript processor.

ELISE RIGGINS, incredibly talented editor.

All mistakes are mine.

Phil Jones

Note to the Reader: <u>Images of America: Hilton Head Island,</u> compiled by editor Natalie Hefter, is a very good book that provided useful information about the Hilton Head story.

# Photographs

Early 1950s- Dad reading to Janice and Phil.

Phil Jones

1954- Phil in jeep.

1954- Phil in jeep with attached trailer.

1954- Jeep and trailer on an omnipresent (often one lane) dirt road. Our jeep frequently rescued cars stuck in the dirt.

Easter 1954- Phil and Dad.

Easter 1954- Phil, Wayne, and Barkey.

1956- Phil and Minnie.

1950s- Oceanside view of house.

1958- Phil on Minnie. Janice on Starlight. Candy Doll home in the background.

1958- Phil, Wayne, and Janice at shower on boardwalk. Dennis in the background at screen porch door.

Phil Jones

Late 1950s- Phil and Dennis sitting on boardwalk.

Cocktails and Prayers

**HILTON HEAD MONKEY**—Dr. W. E. Hoy, head of the University of South Carolina biology department, holds a monkey shot on Hilton Head Island. A study is being made of its means of survival and origin of the tribe in existence there.
(AP Wirephoto)

April 10, 1958- Wirephoto in *The Augusta Chronicle* newspaper of Dr. W.E. Hoy, head of the University of South Carolina Biology Department, as he holds a monkey shot on Hilton Head Island. (Permission was granted to use this photograph.)
70

Phil Jones

Late 1950s- House with Miami windows. Dennis at garage
entrance on a tricycle, clerestory windows are visible over flat
roof.

Early 1960s- Candy Doll preparing supper.

Early 1960s- Shooting clay pigeons (skeet) on the beach. Phil with hand trap (thrower), Wayne with 20 gauge shotgun.

Early 1960s- Phil with hand trap, Dennis with shotgun.

Cocktails and Prayers

Early 1960s- Phil holds shotgun, Wayne holds pellet rifle on the beach.

Early 1960s- House, 1934 Plymouth, and trailer.

Early 1960s- All of the Jones kids are sitting on the boardwalk.

Early 1960s- All of the Jones kids on the boardwalk.

Early 1960s- Phil and Wayne on the boardwalk.

Early 1960s- Phil leaning against 1962 Cadillac. Note
pyracantha trained as an espalier, a hobby of Dad's.

Phil Jones

Early 1960s- Dennis, Wayne, and Phil on the Beach.

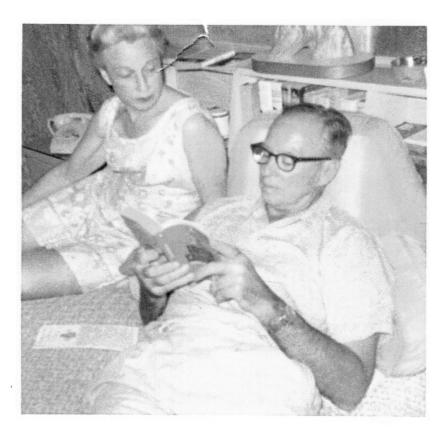

Early 1960s- Dad reading in the bed at Hilton Head with Mom
by his side.

Early 1970s- Mom and Dad.

Early 1970s- Bill and Elizabeth Boyd at Augusta Jones home
for Christmas Eve supper.

Early 1970s- Dad reading in breezeway room.

Early 1970s- Mom seated at the piano in the breezeway room.

1975-Only one of the several banana plants produced fruit.

Cocktails and Prayers

1975-Phil at the end of the boardwalk.

December 25, 1979-Edward Beall prepares breakfast at the
Augusta Jones house. Edward and his wife Roberta did this
every Christmas as their gift to the Joneses.

84

Phil Jones

August 1981-The Jones family has expanded. Representatives from the first, second, and third generation are present in this photograph. Currently, the fourth generation is enjoying our home at the beach.

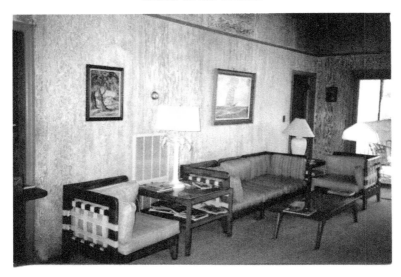

Breezeway room with turquoise furniture
(Dad's first office furniture).

Original kitchen with turquoise cabinets and turquoise beam.

Mom's blonde upright Cable Nelson piano and bench.

Sand fence (to promote dune development), sea oats, beach, sea gulls, and ocean.

Boardwalk with sunlight reflecting over the ocean.

Phil Jones

Moonlight reflecting over the ocean, a guide for loggerhead
turtles and hatchlings back to the ocean.

Palm trees and ocean.

House viewed from Oceanside with portion of boardwalk shown.

Sunrise over the ocean.

Sunrise over the ocean.

Cocktails and Prayers

Sunrise over the ocean. This and the previous two photos were taken by Julie Jones from the boardwalk.

Ocean near high tide, sand fence, and sea oats.

Phil Jones

Ocean at low tide with tidal pool.

CPSIA information can be obtained
at www.ICGtesting.com
Printed in the USA
LVOW05s1550260517

535886LV00006B/6/P